IN CASE OF A FIRE TAKE THE STAIRS

R. R. Black

HOW TO SURVIVE THROUGH DAYS AND NIGHTS

SELF-HELP, POETRY AND REALNESS ALL IN ONE BOOK

MADE SIMPLE.

Library of Congress Control Number: 2019920408

rrblack.com

Instagram:@Incaseofafire_

contact@rrblack.com

© Copyright 2019, R. R. Black

All rights reserved. No part of this book can be produced in any form without written permission from the author.

Paperback

ISBN: 978-1-7342161-4-1

Society constantly wants me to be better
but it's expecting me to do worse

I'm so f*cking sick of being who you expect me to be

I am happiest when I am fed
I am a complete nightmare on a empty stomach

What is closure
Should I forgive and carry on
Or should I carry on this grudge that gives me closure

I've loved you more than all I know
Everyone I know know's you don't
like me

You: I want to lose weight
I want to feel beautiful
I want to be smarter
I want to be more focused
I want the room to stop when I enter
I want heads to turn

Someone else: I want to love you

Why can't my job see my worth
Why can't you see your own worth and quit your job

I've been pretending to laugh at your jokes for far too long

Why am I asked to smile
Are you mad because I simply didn't smile at you
You poor thing seeking a strangers validation

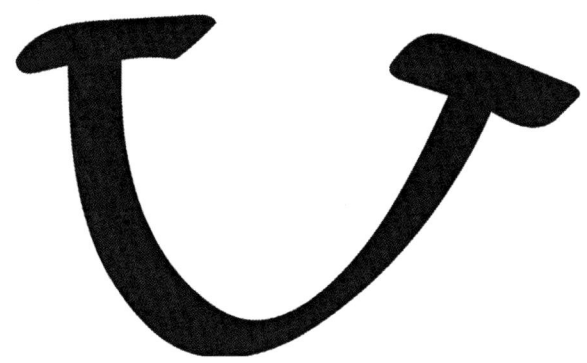

My skin, my body
God's decision
Not yours

You can't be unique if you're just like everyone else

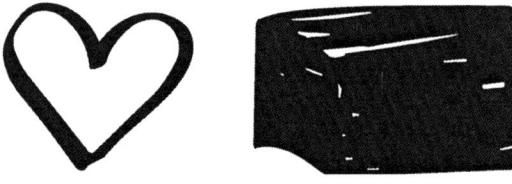

Love is painful usually because it isn't mutual

Let me be clear
My personal boundaries are not to make you feel bound or restricted

---

    My personal boundaries is to control my life my way respectively

Are you feeling empty because you want more for yourself
The key is to need more
If something becomes more vital in your life you'll do everything in your power to fulfill the emptiness within you

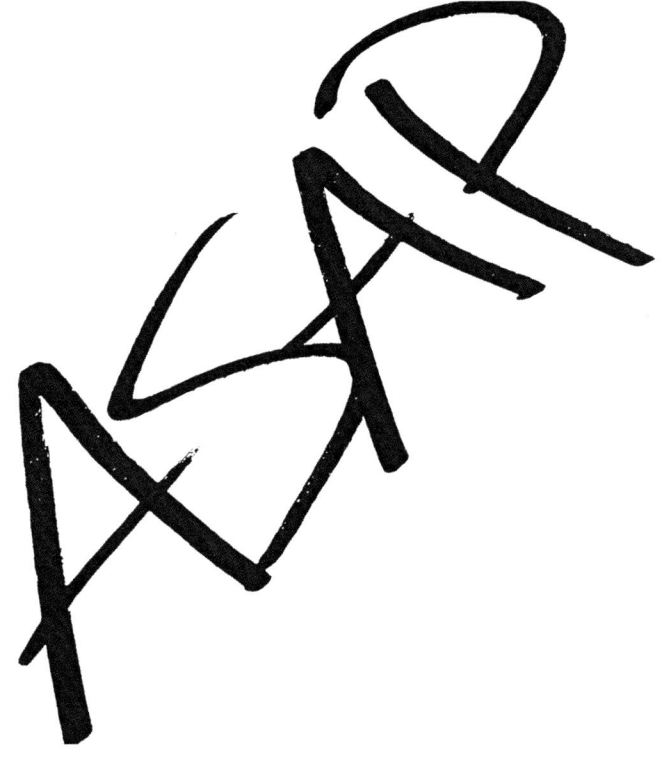

I don't always know my place in this world
So sometimes I just like to be at home

Do you always say that you're okay
Is this the truth or a lie
If it is a lie reevaluate your answer then tell the truth

People will always try to test you
Stay excellent don't give in to the BS

Microaggressions are never flattering

Do at least one good thing for someone else before 12am

Want to know the secret to end chaos in this world
Kindness

Only telling me what I want to hear isn't considered fair nor honest

I will not be overwhelmed today

If you don't ASK you will not GET
If you don't try
It will never happen

You can't complain if you never put in the work to change your situation

When you feel trapped against the wall
Kick a hole in it and make your way out

It is not okay to lie to a child
To lie to a child is to cause trauma
in their adult hood
Lies creates a generational cycle of deceit
Can you relate

Beggars can't be choosers
I don't think we really asked for poverty

Saying that I am doing a great job does not reflect on my pay check

It's okay to say hello in passing

I was always afraid to speak in front of crowds
I was afraid to share my story
I would stumble over my words because I thought you were judging me
I don't care anymore
Say what you want

I am not adorable
I am grown AF

sign here

Don't wait until your idea is perfect to
make it a reality
Make it real and continue to make adjustments in the process
If you wait until your vision is perfect it will almost never reach the light for your audience to see
Nothing is perfect
Remember
flaws are trending

Sorry for what

Some will try to push you to the edge
Once you've finally fallen off
They'll ask if you're okay
Or ask what's got into you
Typical

Being a bully helps no one
Bullying tarnishes characters for both parties
Bullying is not something that only happens in grade school so grow up

Flaws are trending.

(I enjoyed this line enough to give it its own page)
 Oh, add it to back cover

Keep your hands to yourself

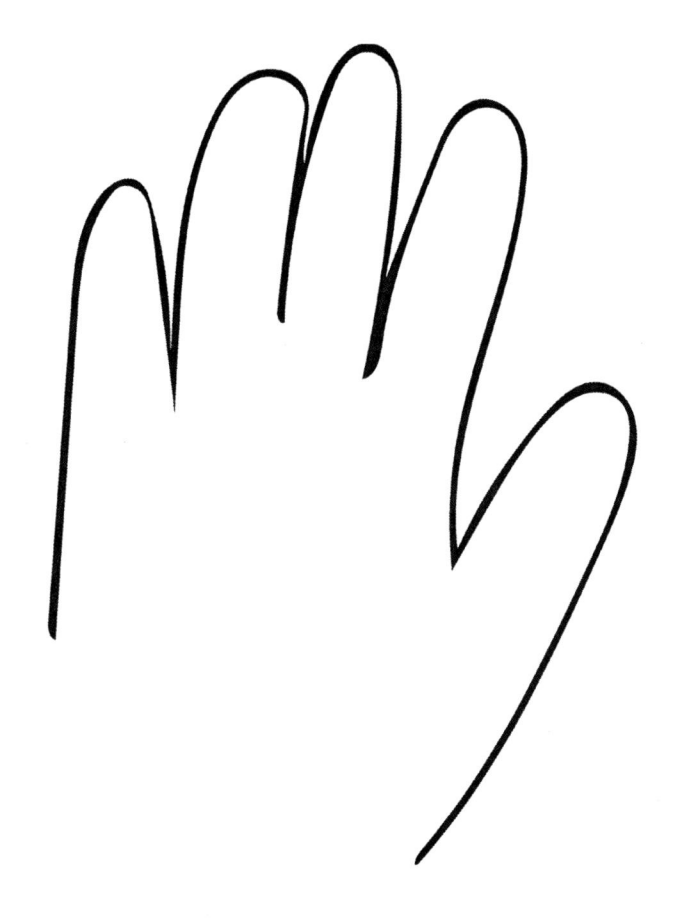

Show love through your actions
I am not in the mood to be manipulated today

I don't get mad for no reason you genuinely hurt me

Look your family in their eyes
You always have your eyes on your
phone looking at families you don't know

Why ask if I need anything
When I finally make a request you want to negotiate

That feeling you get when you check your bank account and you owe over 100 dollars of overdraft fees
Make sure you invest in something with your next paycheck

-100

This mirror can't really reflect what I am feeling right now

Do I look weak to you
Why are you eyeing me so hard from afar
I am not a gazelle
You are a high-five away from getting
your feelings hurt

Today two dishonest people tried to get over on me
All I wanted was my change

Set at least 5 tiny goals each day
You'll be surprised to see what you've
accomplished by the end of this month

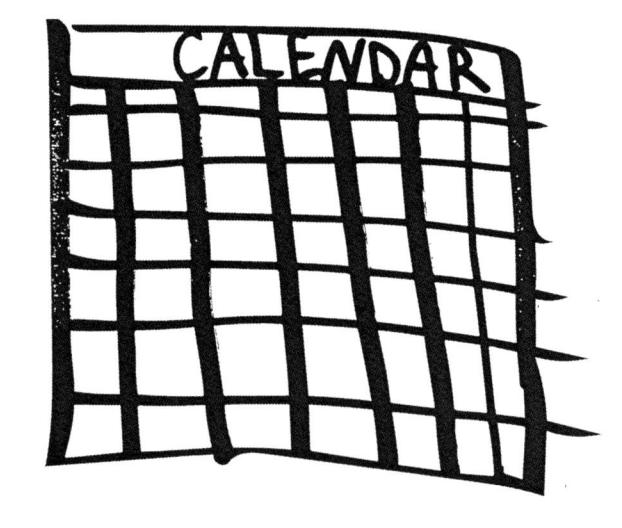

Everything that we do requires initiation and determination
So don't just think about it make productive moves

A luxury car and a hooptie are two very different cars
And yet, they will both get you where you need to go
Life is like that
Doesn't matter how you get to your destination just get there
Show up

(My moma told me this and it genuinely changed my life. I needed to share this advice with you.)

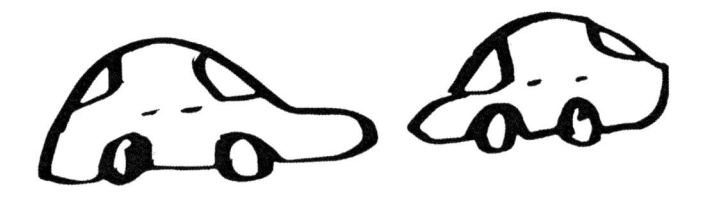

I was told that I was disqualified
I should of applied anyways
Some people can be gate stoppers
Next time deny me on paper

My definition of a gate stopper is someone who tells you no only out of spite, jealousy or envy

You can never have what they have
Get over it and focus on what you want
You'll feel better

Think about what you want to accomplish today
Write a list of your goals below

I have a secret that will bring a little delight in your life
Stop thinking twice
Get that idea accomplished the first time
Second thoughts come with hesitation and doubt
Kick that second thought to the curb

How long are you going to wait for that promotion before you finally promote yourself

Do the same thing get the same results
It's that simple
This can be good or it can be a habit worth eliminating

(My grammy said it best.)

Our minds are like bags of candy
Fill it up to the rim and repeat
Always share

Roth IRA

Google it

Invest in stock
Don't know it
Learn it

Build your credit
Know what for
Invest in something worth a large return

(buy land, property, art etc.)

Network
Community is everything
Trust me

Purchase life insurance
Don't wait until it's too late and your family have to wash cars only to bury you

When one door close another one will open
Some say be ready
I say get in construction worker mode and build that door
When you're done open it yourself

Feeling alone right now
Appreciate this time
Do not take this time for granted
Want to be in a crowd step in a seminar or brainstorm your own big event
Downtime can be used for meditation or creating
People can be headaches or sometimes distractions
Embrace this temporary feeling

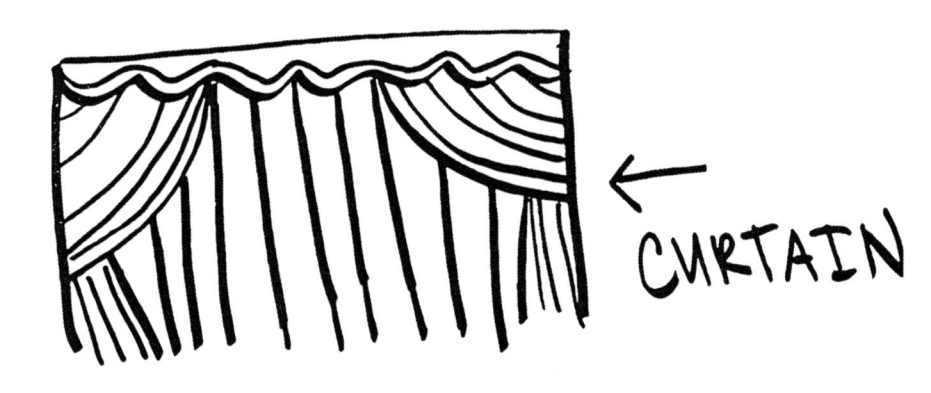

← CURTAIN

How much time have you dedicated for yourself today?

At my most depressed state
The world's appearance changed to black and white
Nothing around me had it's original color chosen by God
I cried even at work without warning
I had no place to go in my mind
I knew I needed help
My best friend recommended therapy
I did not disagree
My therapist recommended
For me to hit the gym
Take a walk in nature
The tree leaves began turning green as I stepped foot into the wilderness
Through meditation and changing my environment I began to gradually heal
My journey is not over yet

Mental health is not a myth

Procrastination is a curable disease
Get healed before it spreads
Antidote: Making it happen

Screaming may turn their heads but it will not make them listen

Unfortunately it's too late to give up now
You are almost there

I've cried myself to sleep at night only to wake up with sore eyes and a fresh start

Choose friends based off their qualities not by the quantity

Everyday you cross paths with someone
You've crossed paths with someone who have lost
Always be polite

An opinion about someone else's appearance has no value

Saying someone look tired is insulting if they aren't
They are probably tired of hearing it

I will not be discouraged today

Anxiety is passing though my veins like quick sand
As I write I feel the numbness in my hands
My heart is beating rapidly without a run
I will continue to breath and keep going

Don't try to change the lover that is good to you
Switch your train of thought of your lover

UNCON
DITION
NAL
LOVE

Tell them the truth.

You deserve better
Make an offer to yourself that you can not refuse

Misery will milk it's company dry

Being self aware is just being knowledgeable of who you are, what you want and how you feel Some of these things will change within our lifetime but don't ever be persuaded enough to forget

If I can't count on you then I can't keep your number

If I can count on you then I can keep your number

When was the last time you've done something that you're passionate about

Things happen in life to squeeze you into your purpose

(From my mom again.)

If you don't know how to say no then just say the complete opposite of yes

NO

When you abandon me you've abandoned yourself
When your lies became let downs
These lies became lost days to get to know me
Moments that could never be replaced
Love, your kid

Travel
Get out there and explore
Go on an adventure
What if all of this truly meant take a trip to the fridge
Explore your options
If there's nothing there order take out from that one place you've always been wanting to try
Kick back on the couch and watch a film
Your mental break might be a bit closer than what you may think

Happiness is meant to be recognized and appreciated when it finally approaches you
Not obsessed over, exploited and forced

Another day lived is another chance to make it right

I saw you walk away today
Once you were out of sight someone exposed a piece of you that you've buried for probably majority of your life
I spoke up for you today
I'm so sorry
We have to respect each other.

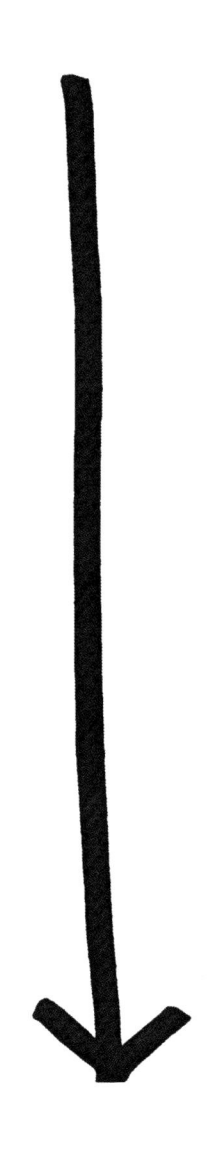

To reach your highest potential is to at least know how far you want to go.

Attention all humans:
Mind your business

Get up
Get it done
Do nothing
Get no results

Don't be afraid
Our minds can really scare us into not taking risks, not speaking up for ourselves or being content
You are worth so much more
Never settle

Stop pretending to be someone you're not in new relationships
When you finally get comfortable and be who you are
They will always say you've changed

It belongs to her
So, why are you mad

How can you kiss the ground that I walk on and walk all over me
If you continue at this pace then I recommend you to walk away

I can not be all of your happy
I'm only human
Or am I only being selfish

Some say be realistic
I like to pretend that I'm a f*cking fairy
That's where the real money is

Step out of that cube that others put you in
Be a circle
Being well rounded is a super power

Inequality
Nah

INEQUALITY NAH

Be a good person
It'll assist with your day

Stop biting your tongue it's only going to bleed

Play your favorite song
Close your eyes and dance that stress away
No one can put on a show like you

go

Obstacles often show off at awful times
We openly feel obligated to   accept losing an opportunity
Or other things may occur
 I say this often
Open your heart to optimism breath and let go

Things aren't always going to work out as planned
So the question is what are you going to do next

No matter how small it is
It's still worth being grateful for

Look in the mirror and say something kind to yourself

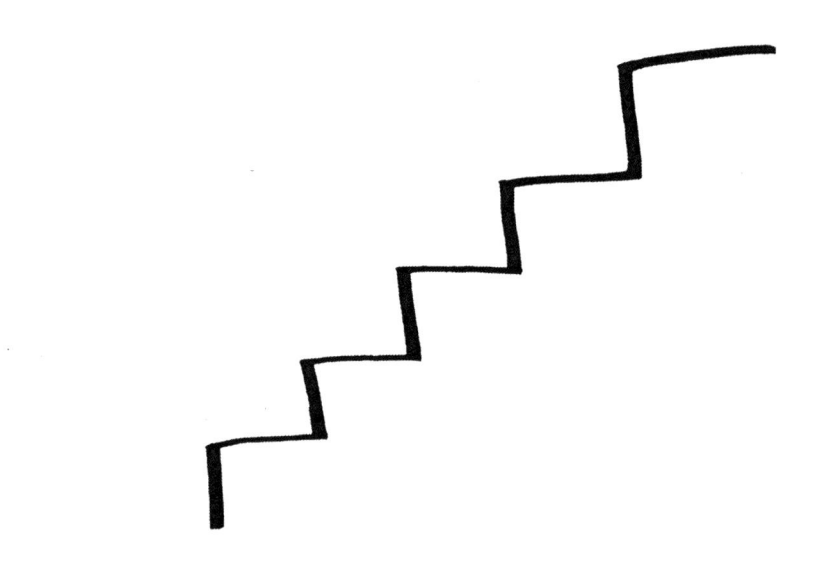

In case of fire take the stairs
We read this often on elevators
I think it's a life's lesson
When things get chaotic in your life
take a new route
When someone brings negativity in your life
move in the opposite direction When you are
the one being the negative person re-evaluate
yourself and take the stairs

Choosing to record an emergency instead of calling for help is not acceptable
It should be an illegal act but that's just my opinion

If you're silent long enough people will begin to show you who they truly are

Today I'm manic
I'm mentally overwhelmed and extremely excited
I'm going to sit on this toilet and breath

You must understand that you don't owe anyone anything
Well, it depends

Parental Guidance is advised.

(What more can I say about this powerful statement?) Be there.

Respect and kindness should be an obligation

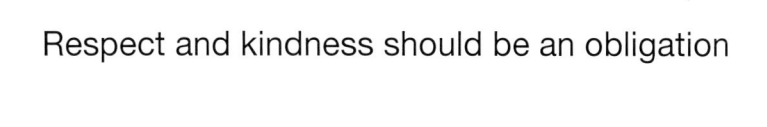

Stop blaming other's for your own f*ck ups
This will assist with your healing

Stop asking your friends for money knowing you'll forget to pay them back
This is unethical

Stop giving money away expecting it back in return
You will get let down almost every time

Real friends invest together

Spa days are great but if you can't afford it at the moment or don't have the time
Play spa music from your phone
Turn your lights off and take a long bath

I scream in my head sometimes
I have a new method of screaming in a pillow to relieve stress
Try it

Dislike your job
Me too

We overthink things too much
Sometime's sh*t is not that complicated

Sometimes I just want good customer service

Saying you need friends to someone who's been there since day one is an insult

That last breakup turned me into an a*shole
Thanks, moving on

Being an introvert is boss
Why? Because you're just being who you are and that's boss

BOSS

Is it possible to be between introverted and extroverted
I mean, I have my days

That exhaustion, heartache and repetition will pass

Sharing my story gave her hope

I have been terrible to the only person who's been good to me
My past have made me reckless today

Show your gratitude and don't take people for granted

How are you feeling?
How was your day?
What can I do to bring joy to your life at this very moment?
Having a good night?
Do you need anything?
Oh, why do I ask?
Well, because I'm just a stranger who genuinely cares
Why is kindness so creepy now of days?

I saw my reflection in your glassy eyes and I couldn't recognize myself

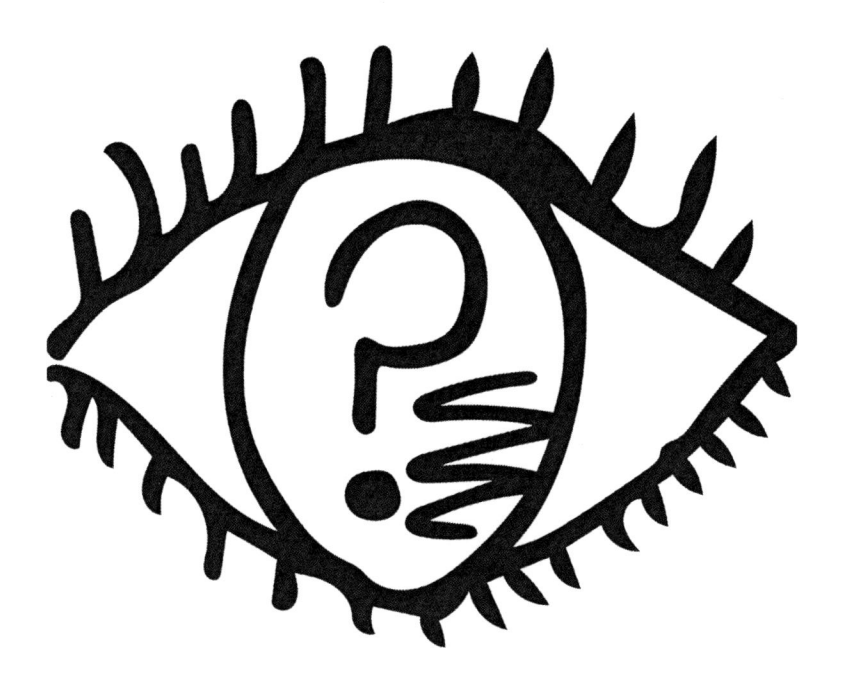

Laughter flowed from my belly harder than any punch in the boxing ring
Thank you for healing me today

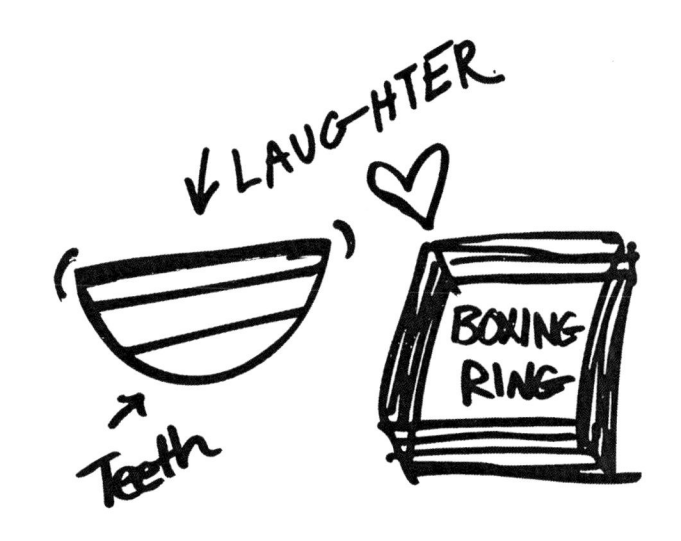

Take a moment to think about what is right not what is wrong

Meditate about it
Pray about it
Talk to someone
Don't let it sit on your heart too long and get stuck in your mind like old gum on a street
Don't let it become you

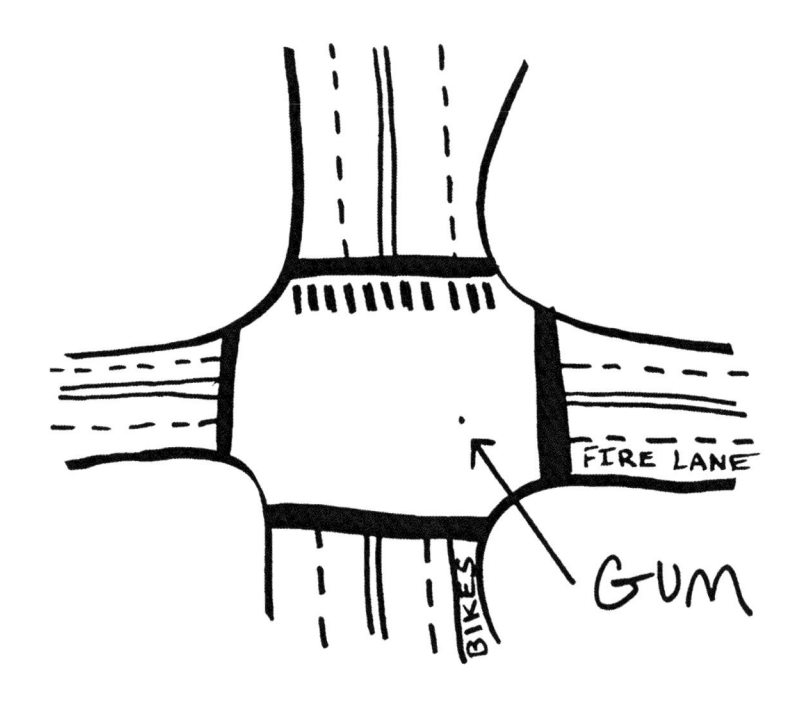

You can not be stuck in one place like these trees

When we gather eat and laugh I feel full of joy

I believed exactly who you were the second you raised your hand

I will not let my fate be determined by your hands

Power is in the tone of your voice and your message behind it

Take a nap

I am not drawn to you based on your looks
I am drawn by the way my heart reacts to your presence

Being envious of the gifts of someone else blinds you from your own

Appreciate the great qualities of others

Speak up for what you deserve

We have to stop being so angry all the time
It's like trying to grow flowers without seeds
If this is caused by other's set expectations and
create boundaries

Believing or not believing is still a belief

Letting my hair nearly hit the bath tubs floor as I listened to the water run from ear to ear
My eyes shifted to the ceiling and I took this time to inhale and exhale to feel my freedom through my breath
In that moment I found peace
In that moment it was just me, the water and my thoughts
A perfect start to my morning
A perfect start to my day

This book is for you but it was written for me
My own truths, realness, metaphors and sarcasm
Straight to the point
Cheer up
A tiny grin goes a long way
This is something we can relate too
This is ours

This book is not intended to solve all your problems only you can
Ask for help if needed
There's so much power in asking for help

Be confident in your work, yourself, your vision and stay persistent

Do it now!

Don't let why's stagnate your awaken dreams

Still don't know what you want to do in life
Then treat your life like a free trial
Test out a few things
If you don't like it cancel it out of your mental subscription

Educate yourself and seek guidance
It is not possible for us to know everything

Success is not always about the money
Do not be misguided

A clean home assists with a clear mind

Our time goes by so fast and we get so busy
Too busy that we don't take the time out for ourselves
Pause and remember to love yourself

I love you.

JOT DOWN YOUR THOUGHTS

You are beautiful and more than capable

Look Moma, Grammy & T I finally completed something. Plus, this book is going to help people!

I dedicate this book to my little brother's heart
I dedicate this book to my baby brother's birth
I dedicate this book to you.

MY SKIN TONE
MIND, BODY,
LAUGHTER, FARTS
AND CRIES
IT IS ALL MINE

rrblack.com

Instagram:@Incaseofafire_

contact@rrblack.com